VOCAL SELECTIONS

TWO BY TWO

Music by
RICHARD RODGERS
Lyrics by
MARTIN CHARNIN
Book by
PETER STONE

Based on "The Flowering Peach" by
CLIFFORD ODETS

T0087394

Photos by ZODIAC PHOTOGRAPHERS, courtesy of Frank Goodman Associates
Original production poster courtesy of Triton Gallery, New York City

Applications for performance of this work, whether legitimate, stock,
amateur, or foreign, should be addressed to:
RODGERS & HAMMERSTEIN THEATRE LIBRARY
229 W. 28 Street, 11th floor
New York, NY 10001

ISBN 0-88188-120-1

7777 W. BLUEMOUND RD. P.O. BOX 13819 MILWAUKEE, WI 53213

TWO BY TWO

Presented by RICHARD RODGERS

Premiere performance November 10, 1970
at the Imperial Theatre, New York

Production Conceived and Directed by JOE LAYTON

Scenery by David Hays
Costumes by Fred Voelpel
Lighting by John Gleason
Musical Direction by Jay Blackton
Orchestrations by Eddie Sauter
Dance and Vocal Arrangements by Trude Rittman

Cast of Characters
(In order of appearance)

Noah...Danny Kaye
Esther ....Joan Copeland
Japheth...Walter Willison
Shem ....Harry Goz
Leah ....Marilyn Cooper
Ham..Michael Karm
Rachel ....Tricia O'Neil
Goldie...Madeline Kahn

THE TIME
Before, during and after the Flood

THE PLACE
ACT I: In and around Noah's home
ACT II: (Forty days and forty nights later)
An ark; and atop Mt. Ararat

Original cast album on Sony Broadway Compact Discs and Tapes

TWO BY TWO

Lyrics by MARTIN CHARNIN

Music by RICHARD RODGERS

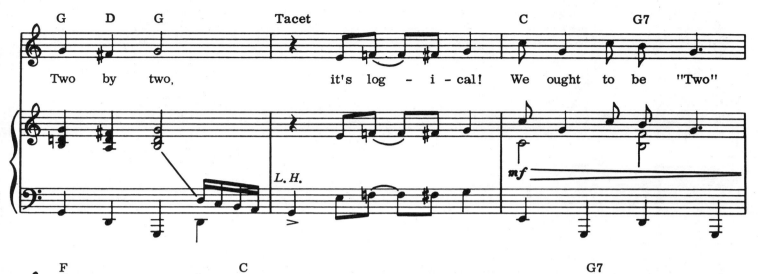

Two by two, it's log - i - cal! We ought to be "Two"

Since we are free to! Sin - gle is grue - some --

Joy - ful is a two - some, ba - by. Two by two, let's make our-selves

Two by two! Don't hes - i - tate, Time we did what

6

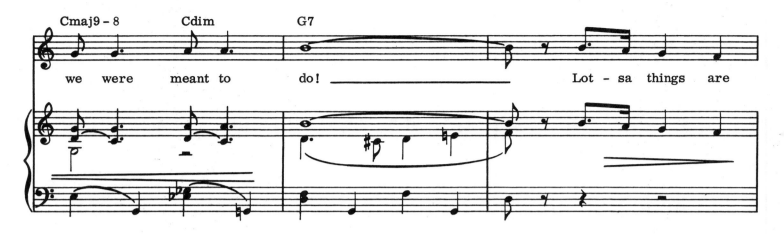

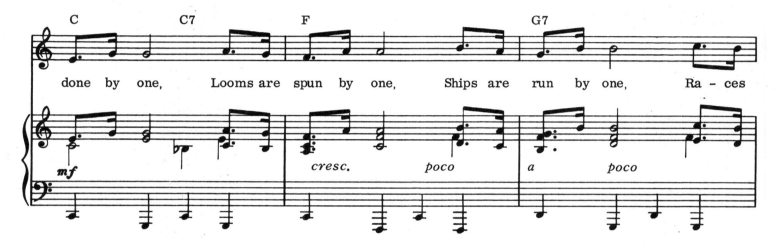

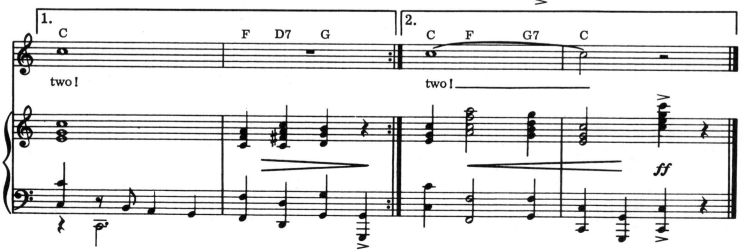

TWO BY TWO

Lyrics by Martin Charnin, from the musical play "TWO BY TWO"

1.

Two by two, the animals,
Two by two, have come to us;
Two by two, just look at 'em,
Two by two, the animals;

Small kinds and fat kinds,
All kinds of cat kinds,
Handsome or gruesome,
Ev'ryone's a twosome, Japhie.

Two by two, it's natural!
Two by two, it's wonderful
Going boating with a floating zoo!

Those who meet God's terms can come,
Pachyderms can come,
Teeny worms can come,
Even germs can come,

If they come together
Two by two.

2.

Two by two, it's logical!
Two by two, it's comf'table!
Two by two, it's catchy, no?
Two by two, it's practical!

God has decreed, "Two,"
Therefore you need to!
Ham's got, and Shem's got,
Go and get what them's got, Japhie.

Two by two, go make yourself
Two by two, and climb aboard.
Plenty room for you and you know who!

Lotsa things are done by one,
Looms are spun by one,
Races are won by one,
Ships are run by one.

When it comes to fam'lies,
Two by two.

3.

Two by two, the creepers are,
Two by two, the crawlers are,
Two by two, the fliers are,
Two by two, the brothers are!

Donkeys and monkeys
All brought their bunkies!
Camels and crickets
All got fam'ly tickets, Japhie.

Two by two, don't hesitate,
Two by two, it's time that you
Did what me and Momma used to do!

Will ya hug and smooch? Ya will!
Betcha boot ya will.
If she's cute, ya will,
Feel so mutual.

In a bed, it's better
"Two by two."

4.

Two by one, is mizz'rable!
Two by two is sensible!
Two by three is possible!
Two by four is dangerous!

Gooses and grouses
All brought their spouses.
Blonde or brunette one,
Japhie, go and get one, Japhie.

Two by two, you'll learn a lot.
Two by two, you'll smile a lot.
Someone there to care to see you through.

Every kind of male that's here,
From the snail that's here
To the quail that's here,
To the whale that's here,

Has to pair off. They're off!
Two by two.

You Have Got To Have A Rudder On The Ark

Lyrics by MARTIN CHARNIN

Music by RICHARD RODGERS

leaf up - on a tree; _____ And I'm cer - tain you'll ad -
clothes or else you freeze; _____ And I know you will a -
have a lot of teeth; _____ And no mat - ter how you

mit that an ap - ple needs a pit, And there's got to be a
gree that a lock should have a key, And a pea soup has to
try, e - ven you can - not de - ny, That a top has got to

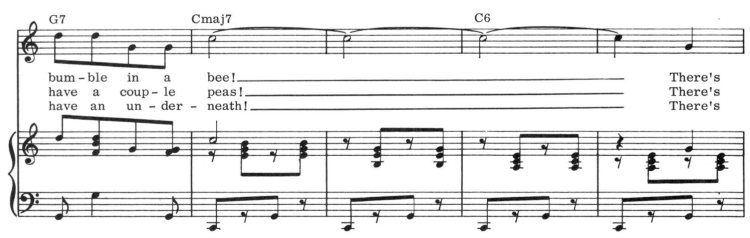

bum - ble in a bee! _____ There's
have a coup - le peas! _____ There's
have an un - der - neath! _____ There's

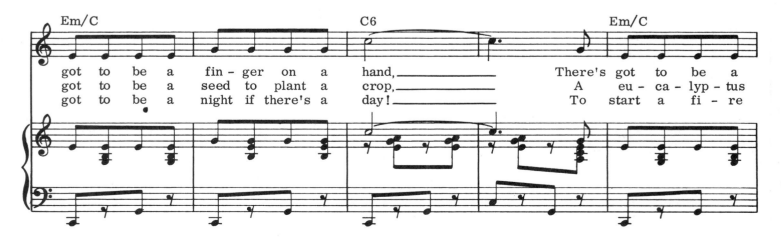

got to be a fin - ger on a hand, _____ There's got to be a
got to be a seed to plant a crop, _____ A eu - ca - lyp - tus
got to be a night if there's a day! _____ To start a fi - re

light to change the dark;_____ Like the fin-ger and the bum-ble, and no
has to have a bark;_____ Like the tear drop and the win-ter, stop the
you must have a spark;_____ Pop-pa, give in; Pop-pa, face it, let us

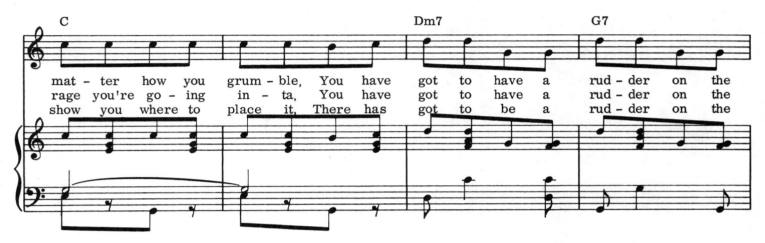

mat-ter how you grum-ble, You have got to have a rud-der on the
rage you're go-ing in-ta, You have got to have a rud-der on the
show you where to place it, There has got to be a rud-der on the

ark!_____ You have got to have a rud-der
ark!_____ You have got to have a rud-der
ark!_____ You have got to have a rud-der

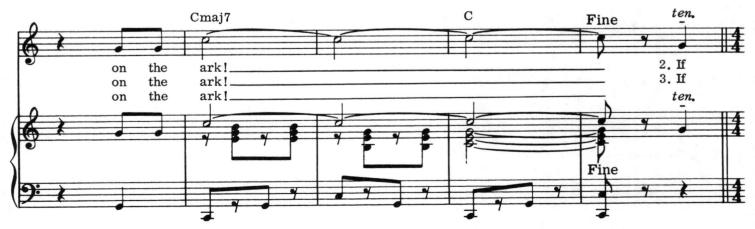

on the ark!_____ 2. If
on the ark!_____ 3. If
on the ark!_____

SOMETHING DOESN'T HAPPEN

Lyrics by MARTIN CHARNIN

Music by RICHARD RODGERS

Moderato

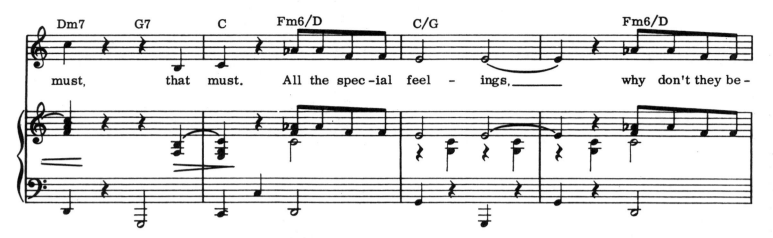

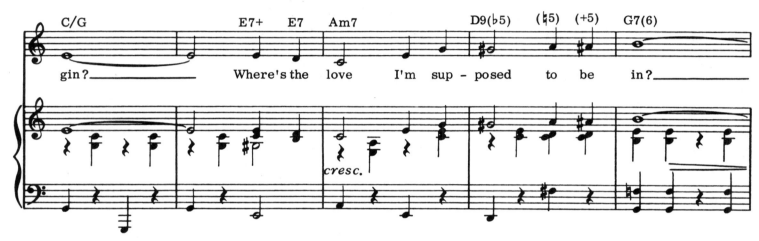

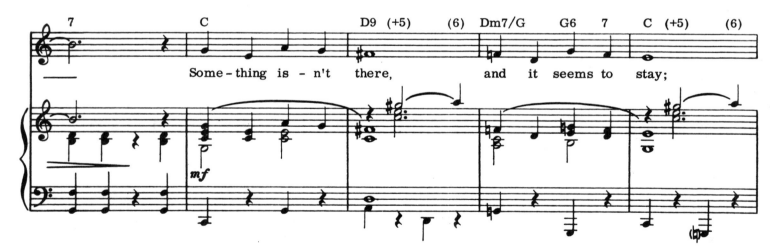

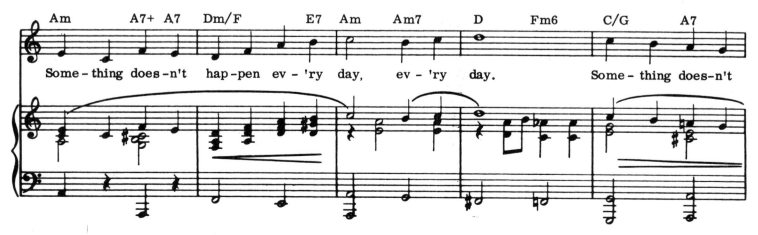

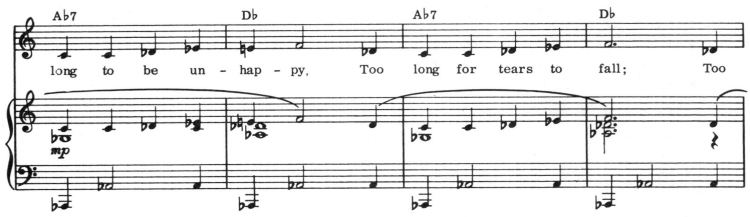

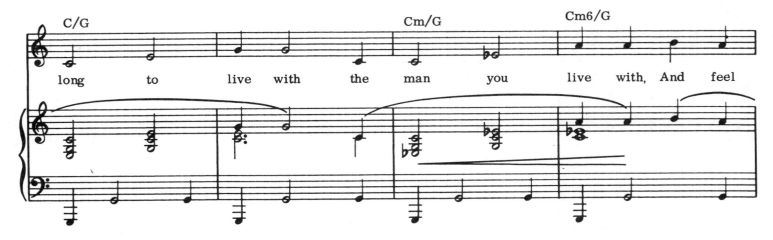

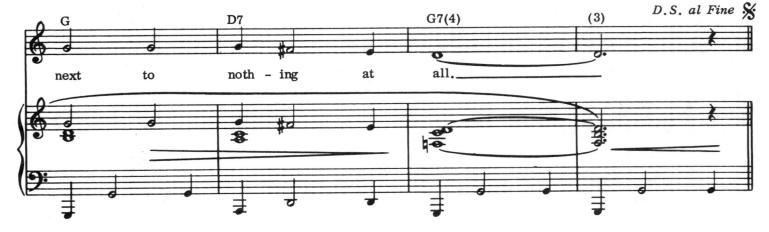

AN OLD MAN

Lyrics by MARTIN CHARNIN

Music by RICHARD RODGERS

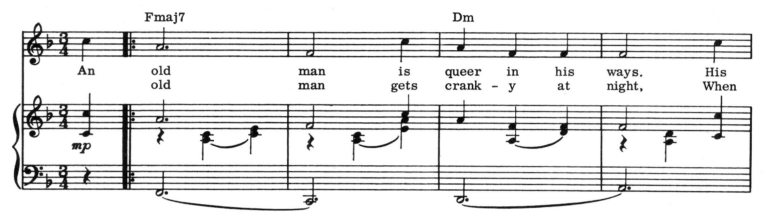

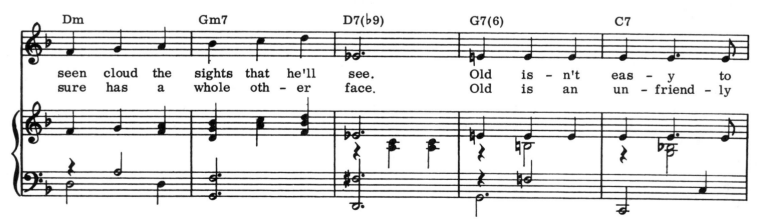

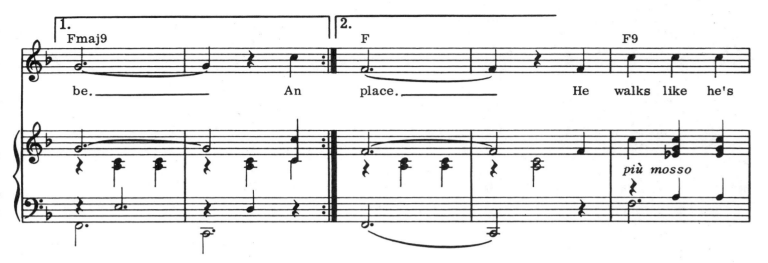

be. _____ An place. _____ He walks like he's

più mosso

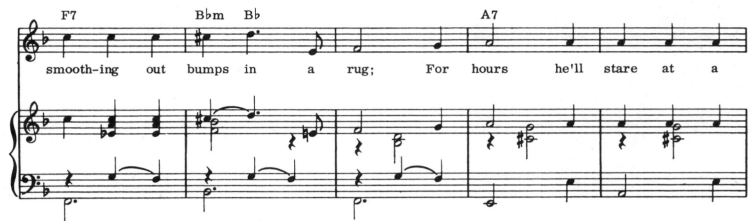

smooth-ing out bumps in a rug; For hours he'll stare at a

spot; _____ The hug that he gives you is hard - ly a

hug. (You re - mem - ber the hug that it's not an - y - more.) An

poco rit.

Tempo I

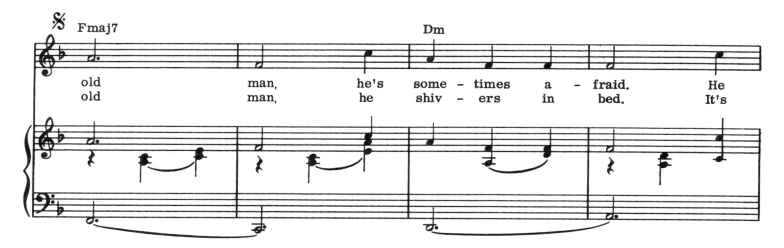

old man, he's some - times a - fraid. He
old man, he shiv - ers in bed. It's

sings to the sun, But he's par - tial to shade; To him-
all of the years that have spun 'round his head. He's the

self he's a wit, To the world he's a pest.
bur - den - some thing that a world fam - 'ly ig -

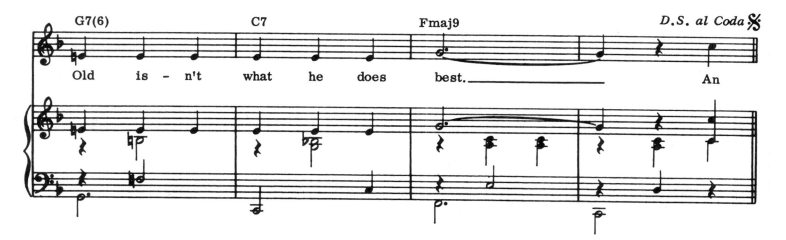

Old is - n't what he does best. _____ An

D.S. al Coda

Coda ⊕

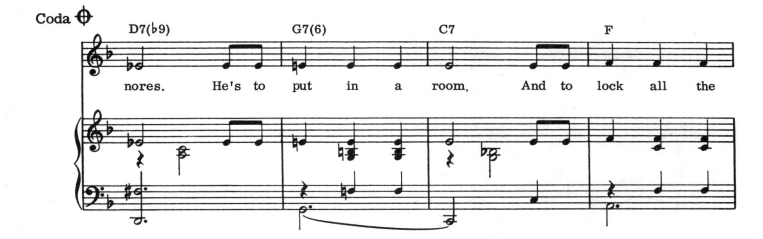

nores. He's to put in a room, And to lock all the

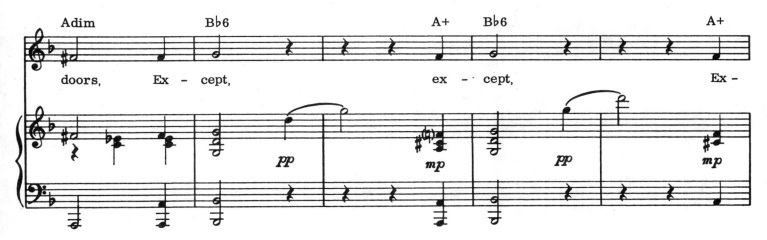

doors, Ex - cept, ex - cept, Ex -

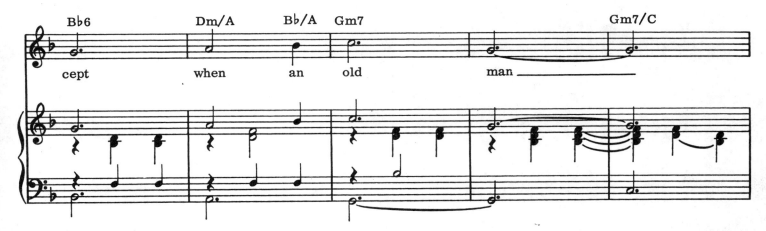

cept when an old man _____

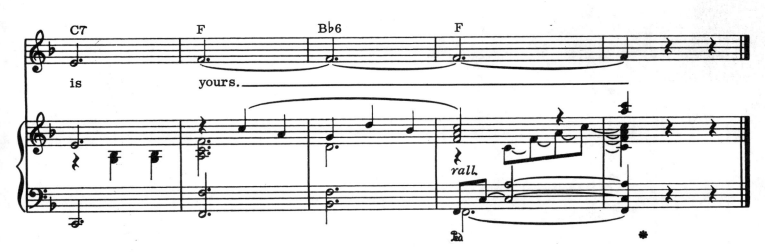

is yours. _____

WHEN IT DRIES

Lyrics by MARTIN CHARNIN

Music by RICHARD RODGERS

1. Why are you so gloom - y? We're a -
4. Half a mil - lion grow - ing things will
7. Grate - ful to sur - vive, we'll all live

live and we're a - float. Af - ter for - ty days and nights it's ship - shape on the
spring up from the ground. Half a mil - lion bod - ies will be float - ing all a -
side by side in peace, Car - ing for the an - i - mals and watch - ing them in -

boat. Look! The sun's come out a - gain and turned a ros - y red.
round. Room to work and grow and build a com - pa - ny of men,
crease. Is - n't it a mir - a - cle, a brand new world be - gins!

F7 / Bb / Bb7

How can you be gloom-y when you think of what's a-head? 2. It's
Think a-bout how much we can con-ta-mi-nate a-gain! 5. There's
Think of all the fun we'll have, in-vent-ing brand new sins! 8. We're

Allegretto

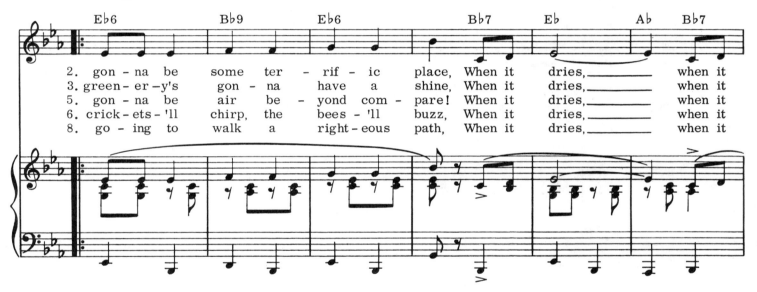

Eb6 / Bb9 / Eb6 / Bb7 / Eb / Ab / Bb7

2. gon-na be some ter-rif-ic place, When it dries,_____ when it
3. green-er-y's gon-na have a shine, When it dries,_____ when it
5. gon-na be air be-yond com-pare! When it dries,_____ when it
6. crick-ets-'ll chirp, the bees-'ll buzz, When it dries,_____ when it
8. go-ing to walk a right-eous path, When it dries,_____ when it

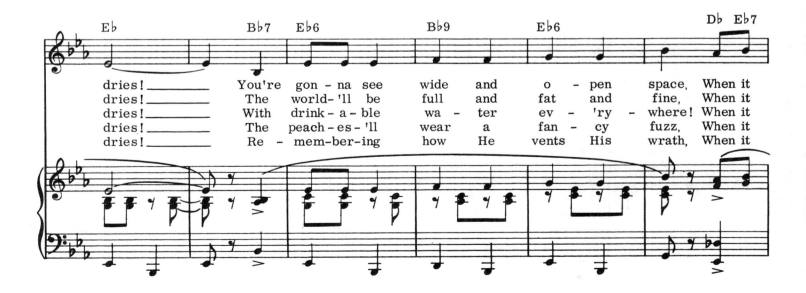

Eb / Bb7 / Eb6 / Bb9 / Eb6 / Db / Eb7

dries!_____ You're gon-na see wide and o-pen space, When it
dries!_____ The world-'ll be full and fat and fine, When it
dries!_____ With drink-a-ble wa-ter ev-'ry-where! When it
dries!_____ The peach-es-'ll wear a fan-cy fuzz, When it
dries!_____ Re-mem-ber-ing how He vents His wrath, When it

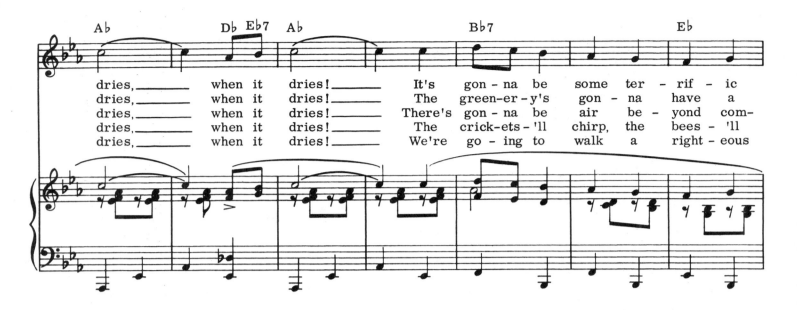

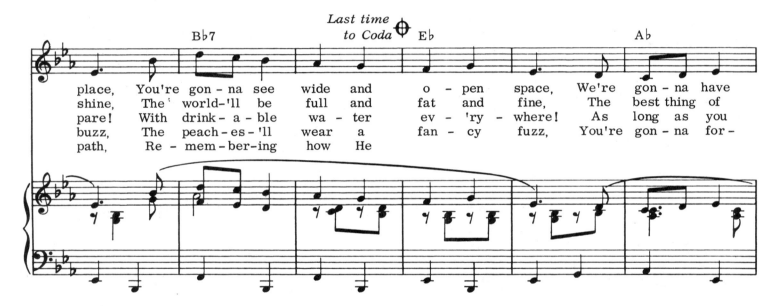

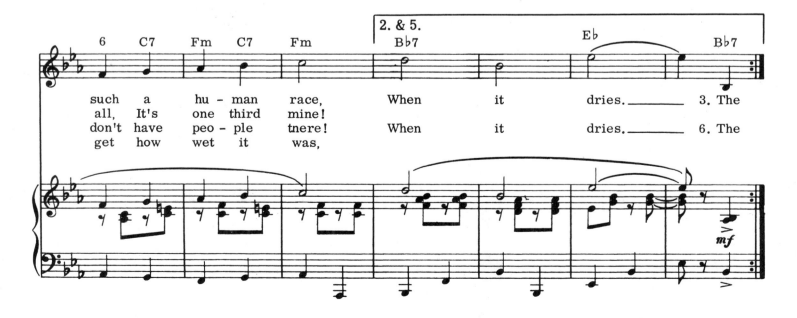

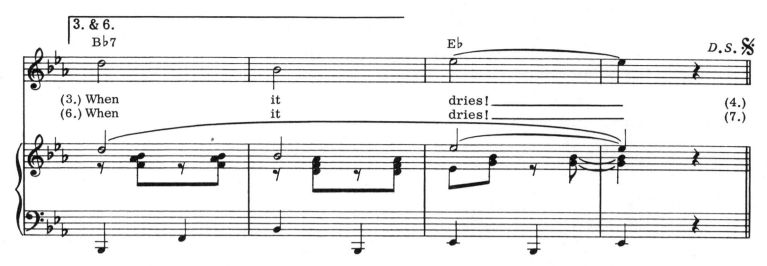

3. & 6.

Bb7   Eb   *D.S.* 𝄋

(3.) When   it   dries!   (4.)
(6.) When   it   dries!   (7.)

Coda ⊕

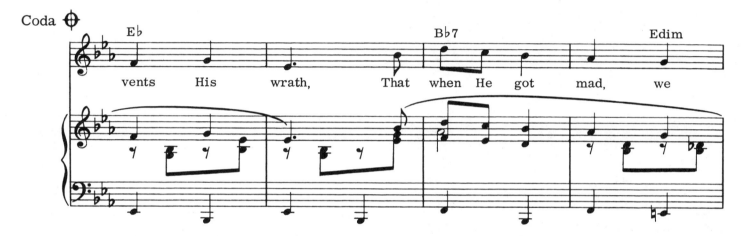

Eb   Bb7   Edim

vents   His   wrath,   That   when   He   got   mad,   we

Fm   Dbdim   Fm   C7   F7   Bb7.

took   some   bath!   When   it

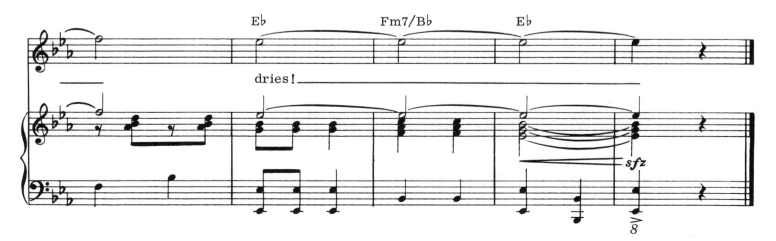

Eb   Fm7/Bb   Eb

dries!   *sfz*

8

HEY, GIRLIE

Lyrics by MARTIN CHARNIN

Music by RICHARD RODGERS

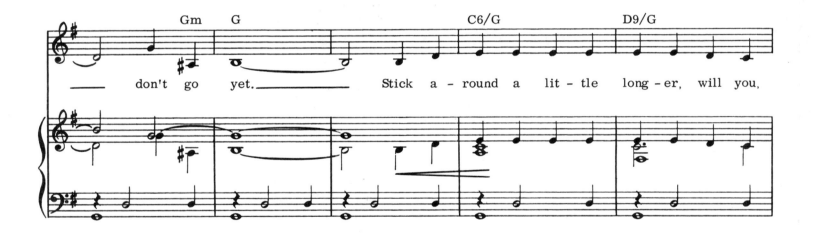

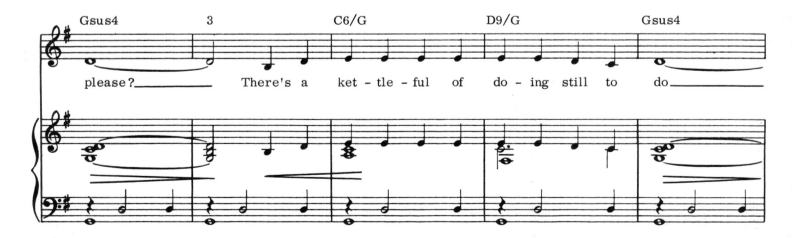

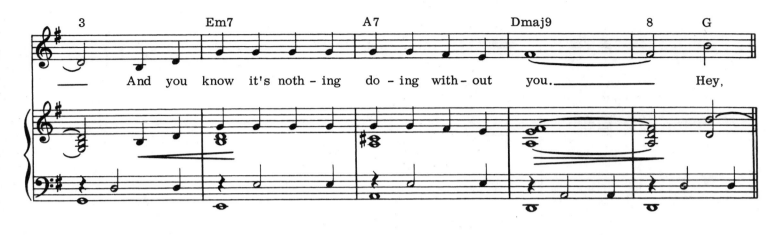

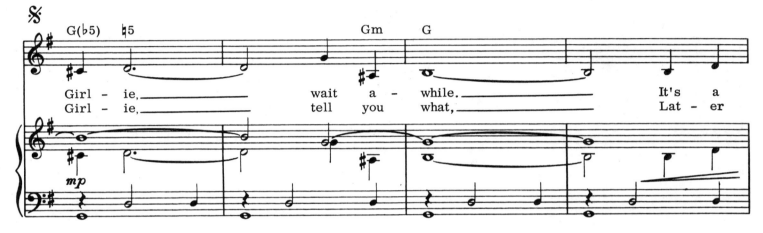

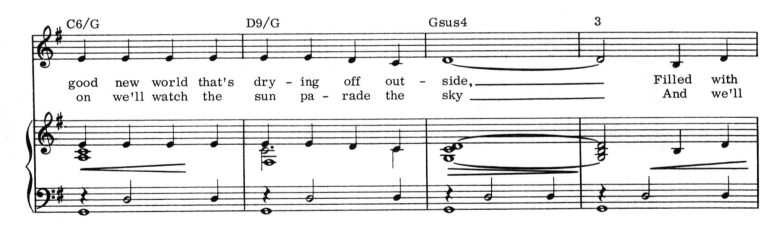

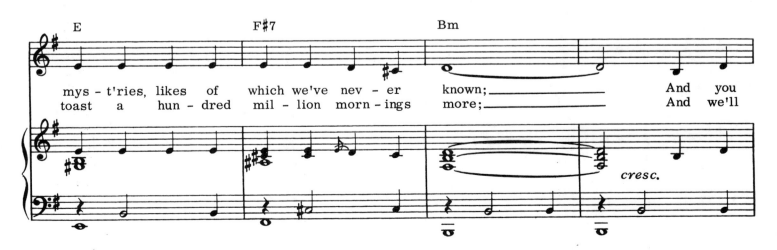

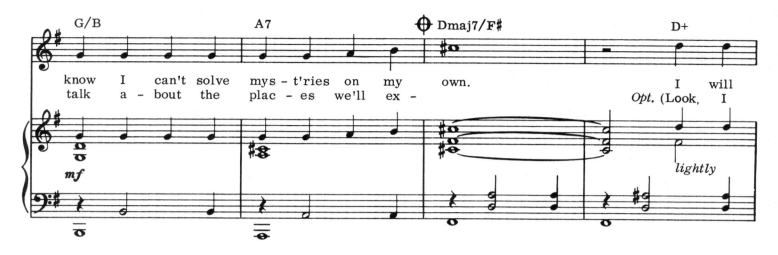

know I can't solve mys - t'ries on my own.
talk a - bout the plac - es we'll ex -

Opt. (Look, I

I will

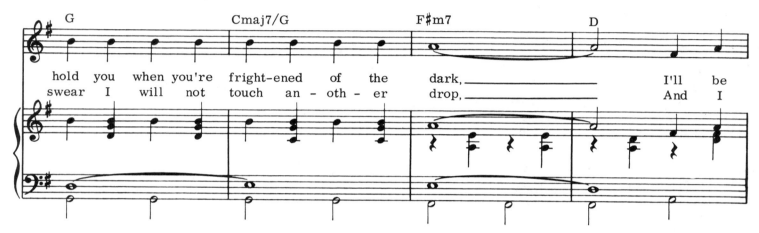

hold you when you're fright-ened of the dark,
swear I will not touch an - oth - er drop,

I'll be
And I

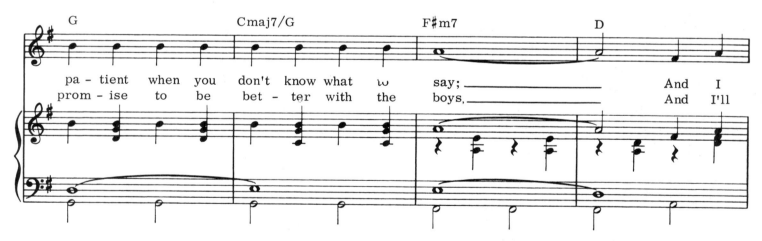

pa - tient when you don't know what to say;
prom - ise to be bet - ter with the boys,

And I
And I'll

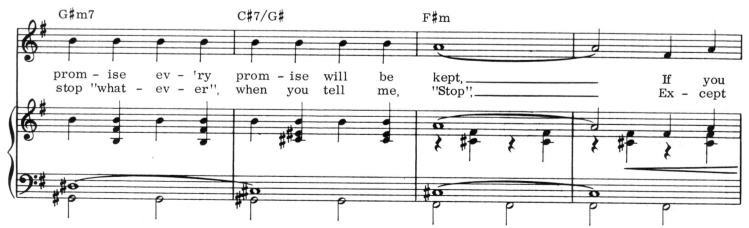

prom - ise ev - 'ry prom - ise will be kept,
stop "what - ev - er", when you tell me, "Stop",

If you
Ex - cept

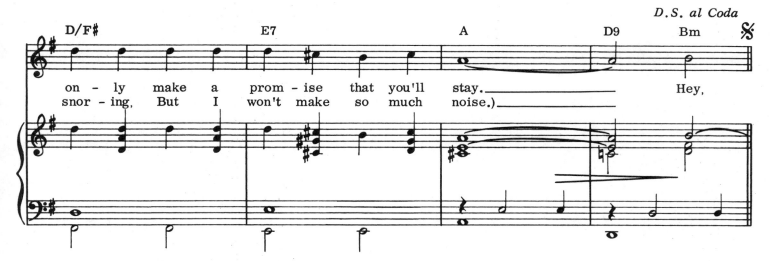

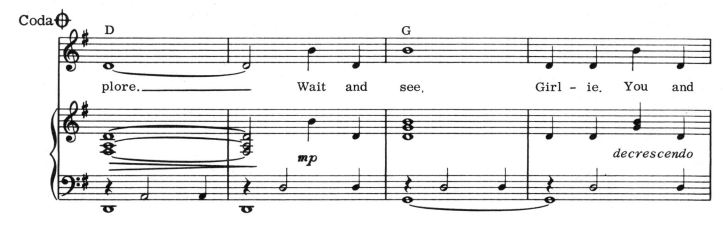

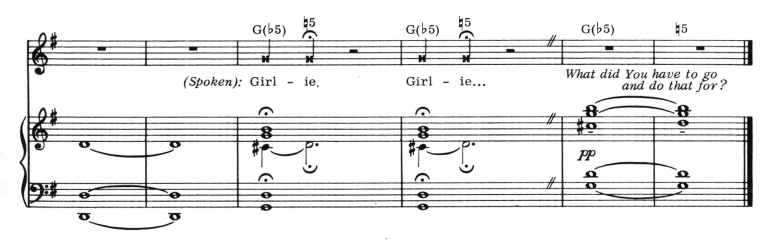

SOMETHING, SOMEWHERE

Lyrics by MARTIN CHARNIN

Music by RICHARD RODGERS

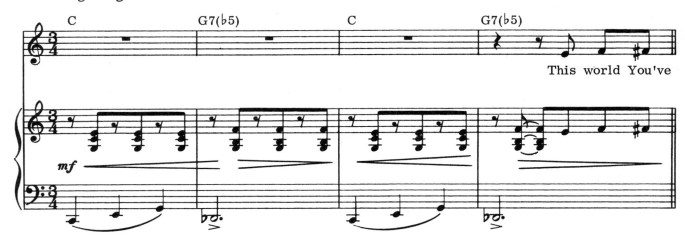

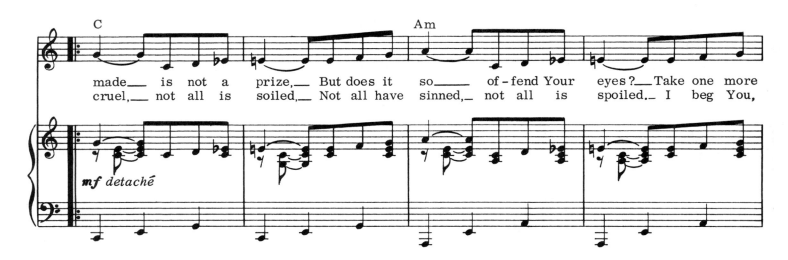

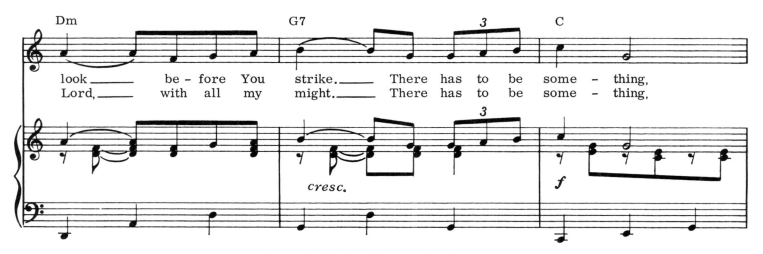

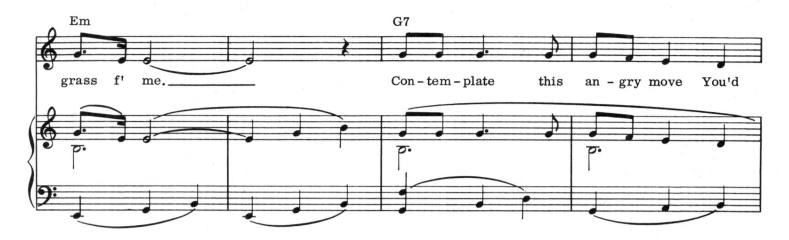

grass f' me._____ Con-tem-plate this an-gry move You'd

make._____ Lord I love, I run the risk of

blas-phe-my!_____ But this thing You do is a mis-

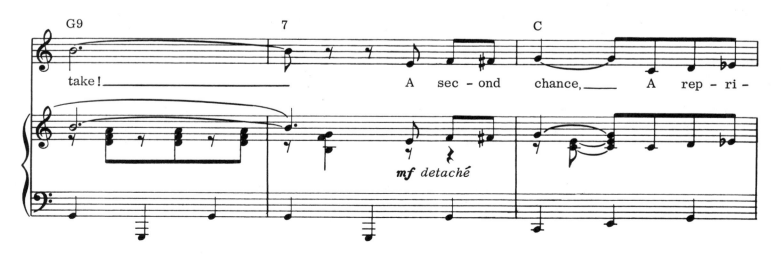

take!_____ A sec-ond chance,_____ A rep-ri-

YOU

Lyrics by **MARTIN CHARNIN**

Music by **RICHARD RODGERS**

Moderato (with a lilt)

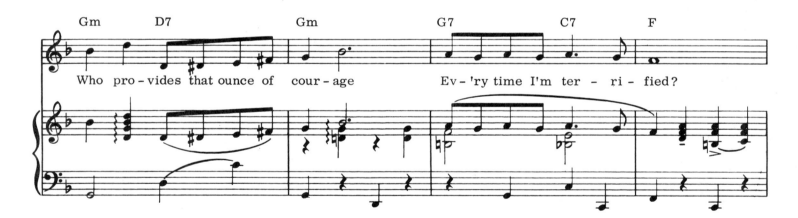

Who is al-ways in my cor - ner? Who is al-ways at my side?

Who pro-vides that ounce of cour - age Ev-'ry time I'm ter - ri - fied?

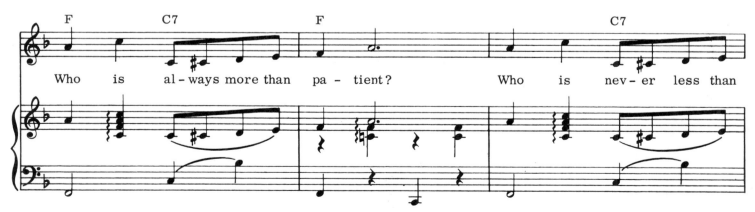

Who is al-ways more than pa - tient? Who is nev-er less than

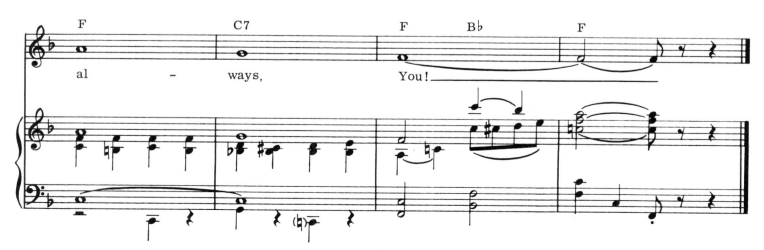

I Do Not Know A Day I Did Not Love You

Lyrics by MARTIN CHARNIN

Music by RICHARD RODGERS

har-vest, when the sun danced in your hair._____ I do not know a day I did not need you _____ For shar-ing ev-'ry mo-ment that I spent._____ I need-ed you be-fore I ev-er knew you,

_____ Be- fore I knew what need-ing some - one meant._____ And

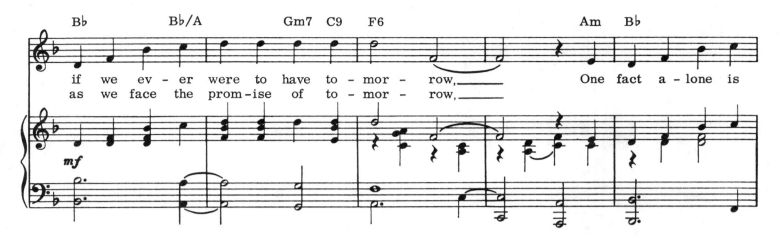

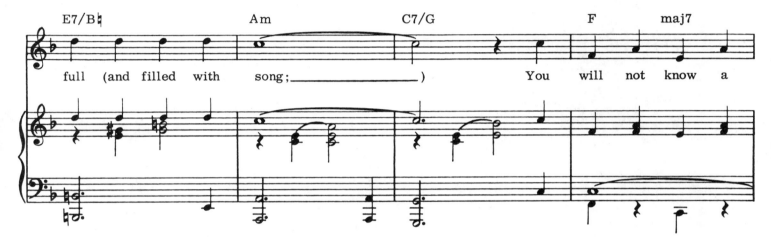

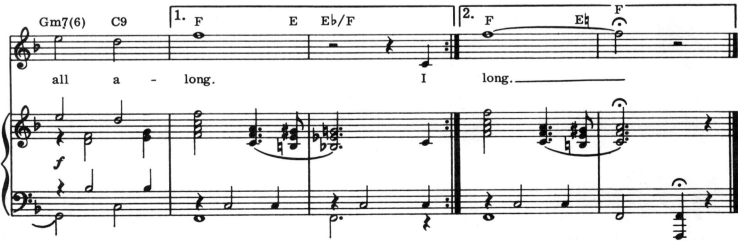